Pied Piper

Musical activities to develop basic skills

John Bean and Amelia Oldfield

Jessica Kingsley Publishers
London and Philadelphia

The right of John Bean and Amelia Oldfield to be identified as authors of this work has been asserted by them in accordance with the Copyright, Designs and Patents Act 1988.

First published in United Kingdom in 1991 by
Cambridge University Press

Published in the United Kingdom in 2001 by
Jessica Kingsley Publishers Ltd,
116 Pentonville Road, London
N1 9JB, England
and
325 Chestnut Street,
Philadelphia PA 19106, USA.

www.jkp.com

© Copyright 2001 John Bean and Amelia Oldfield

Illustrations by Gabrielle Stoddart
Illustrations © Copyright 1991 Cambridge University Press

Library of Congress Cataloging in Publication Data
A CIP catalog record for this book is available from the Library of Congress

British Library Cataloguing in Publication Data
A CIP catalogue record for this book is available from the British Library

ISBN 1 85302 994 7

Printed and Bound in Great Britain by
Athenaeum Press, Gateshead, Tyne and Wear

Contents

Introduction

Why music?

Every day, people make use of music and sound for specific purposes without, perhaps, being consciously aware of it. We raise our voices to gain attention, or sound the car horn to warn other road users. We sing a quiet lullaby to calm a crying child. A signature tune on the radio or the television alerts us to a particular programme.

One obvious use of music is for dancing. Less obviously, we may often find ourselves tapping out a rhythm without having made a conscious effort to do so.

These examples of spontaneous daily reactions to music can be seen in people of all ages and types, including those with disabilities and disorders. People with physical disabilities may not be able to dance or tap their feet, but music still makes them want to move in some way. People with severe learning difficulties do not need to recognize the instruments or the performers in order to feel relaxed when listening to a soothing song.

It is therefore not surprising that music is used in some form or another by many parents, teachers, nurses and therapists to help people with learning difficulties overcome problems.

Purpose of the book

The purpose of *Pied Piper* is to provide ideas of music activities that can be used with a variety of groups.

Traditional music activities such as singing or rhythm games may not be possible or satisfying when working with people with learning difficulties. In this book the emphasis is on *using* music rather than *learning* songs or rhythms. So in most of the activities it is irrelevant how skilled group members are. Many of the activities explore music and sound in very basic ways, and the emphasis is often on helping participants to listen in new ways.

Who can benefit?

The different music activities are deliberately not labelled as suitable for particular client groups. Readers should use their own judgement when selecting activities, and it will often be necessary to adapt an activity slightly to meet the needs of a particular group.

These activities, if chosen carefully, are suitable for children and adults with a wide range of special needs. Many of them can also be used successfully with children in playgroups.

Background

Pied Piper has developed from the authors' experiences as music therapists in the fields of health and education over many years; both have worked with children and adults of all ages and with a wide range of disabilities and disorders. All the activities have been used effectively on many occasions. They will be of use to teachers, nurses, occupational therapists, speech therapists and physiotherapists.

Both authors feel that although music can be used purposefully by many different members of staff, people using these activities should realize that they are not 'doing' music therapy or becoming music therapists themselves. Music therapists are specially trained musicians and their training takes a minimum of four years in the UK.

The book is therefore designed to encourage people to develop their own musical ideas and activities. It is not a manual of music therapy techniques.

How to use the book

Group leaders should clarify the non-musical objectives for each person before selecting an activity. The 'principal aim' and 'further aims' at the beginning of each activity will then help them to select appropriately for the needs of their group. Group leaders with limited experience of these types of activity will find it useful to plan sessions carefully, keeping them short and simple. It must be remembered, however, that activities are not formulae guaranteed to achieve particular aims; they are simply another approach to the problem presented.

The 'variations' suggested indicate the flexibility of each activity and these can be developed to suit the needs of particular groups.

It is important to present a confident approach when singing or playing instruments, even if one lacks experience and feels self-conscious. This may be difficult at first, but practice beforehand can often help. Another way to boost confidence is to use a tambour or tambourine as an accompaniment to singing. It may be helpful to remember that one is not performing as such, but helping people in various ways through music.

However simple the activity presented, it should be well thought out and presented in a quiet, calm environment. Silence and concentrated listening often play an important part, even if at other times loud, exuberant music-making has priority. It is often helpful to keep talking to a minimum and to concentrate particularly on listening to the sounds being produced.

How the book is organized

The activities are divided into four sections according to the principal aim. In each section the more basic activities requiring fewest skills from the participants are presented first, and those requiring more skills are presented last. For planning purposes, group leaders may wish to know at a glance which activities are suitable for wheelchairs or how much equipment is needed, so the authors have included a 'cross-reference' grid at the end of the book to make this easier. A table showing both 'principal aims' and 'further aims' for each activity is also included.

Equipment

Most of the activities do not require a great deal of equipment. It is important though to use good quality instruments that produce clear and rewarding sounds. Instruments should be handled with care, and people should be encouraged to treat them with respect. It is better to have one good quality tambour, for example, than a selection of tinny tambourines and small bells.

The majority of the instruments should be available from local music shops dealing in educational instruments; it is also worth consulting educational catalogues.

Printed tunes

Some activities have tunes printed, in order to help the group leader. Guitar chords, which are in capital letters, are kept to a minimum of only two or three per tune. The notes are also written in, in small letters, to help the leader identify the tune, if necessary, on a keyboard.

The following charts show how six chords are fingered on the guitar. The black dots represent fingers on the strings, and the numbers indicate which fingers should be used.

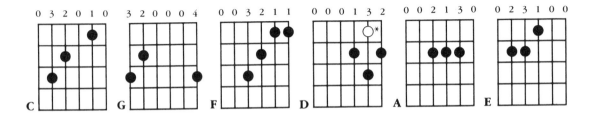

* Use ◯ for D7 instead of ●. The fingering also changes to read, from left to right, 2 1 3

Instruments used in the activities

The following illustration should help readers identify the instruments used in this book and provide ideas for different instruments that can be used.

1 Glockenspiel	11 Keyboard	20 Flexitone	29 Chime bar
2 Chocolo (shaker)	12 Cabasa	21 Guitar	30 Cymbal on string
3 Maraca	13 Xylophone	22 Bells	31 Metronome
4 Auto-harp	14 Cymbal	23 Cuckoo	32 Woodblock
5 Wood-drum (gato drum)	15 Timp tom	24 Horn	33 Chinese woodblock
6 Hand-chimes	16 Swanee flute	25 Metallophone	34 Clappers
7 Kazoo	17 Tambour (hand-drum)	26 Duck-call	35 Penny whistle
8 Indian cymbals	18 Bongo drums	27 Mouth organ	36 Finger cymbals
9 Tambourine	19 Melodica	28 Train whistle	37 Reed horn
10 Guiro (scraper)			

Authors' Acknowledgements

We would like to thank the many therapists and teachers whose workshops stimulated new ideas; also the children, residents, staff and parents of
- the Child Development Centre, Addenbrookes
- the Ida Darwin Hospital
- Douglas House Children's Unit, Cambridge
- the Special Schools in Leicestershire

who took part in the music therapy sessions and provided ideas for new activities. Finally, many thanks to the Cambridge Health Authority, the Leicestershire Education Authority and its School of Music for encouraging the development of this work.

We would like to express our gratitude to Alison Bean for her original sketches, which provided great inspiration for the authors, and served as a basis for Gabrielle Stoddart's delightful pen-and-ink drawings.

Many thanks also to R. Bradley, A. Smalley and to the Addenbrookes Department of Medical Photography (in particular to Ms K. Haslam) for taking some of the photographs:

Hands up! *Roger Bradley*
Conductor *Roger Bradley*
Kings and Queens of the bells *Ms K. Haslam*
Listen and Walk! *Anna Smalley*
Roll to say hello! *Ms K. Haslam*
Lead the leader! *Anna Smalley*

I Activities to develop listening and concentration

Hands up!

Find the leader!

1 Hands up!

PRINCIPAL AIM   To speed up reactions.

FURTHER AIMS
- To develop listening skills.
- To increase concentration.

EQUIPMENT   A small instrument for each group member. A keyboard or recorded music.

NUMBERS   3 to 10.

BASIC MODEL   Each person has an instrument. The leader plays some music, either on a prepared tape or on a keyboard. Whilst the music is playing, everyone joins in with an instrument. When the music stops, all instruments must immediately be held above the head, without a sound. The music can start up again once the group is completely silent.

OBSERVATIONS
- The focus of this activity is observing the silence whilst holding up the instrument. The leader should help the group concentrate on achieving this rather than on the playing.
- The leader can encourage the group by putting up his or her hands as soon as the music stops.

VARIATIONS
- Participants can place their instruments on the floor before raising their hands.

2 Find the leader!

PRINCIPAL AIM	To develop listening skills and concentration.
FURTHER AIMS	• To develop observational skills. • To develop awareness of different group members and their names. • To encourage group initiative.
EQUIPMENT	One tambour.
NUMBERS	3 to 8.
BASIC MODEL	The group sits on chairs in a circle with the leader outside the circle. The leader walks around the group singing and playing the tambour. Suddenly the leader bends down and hides behind one member of the group. The leader remains silent at first, but may play the tambour if he or she is not found quickly. Once the leader is found, participants are asked to name the person behind whom he or she is hidden. When this is done the game starts again.

OBSERVATIONS	• Less verbal or more reticent participants may need encouragement to name other group members.
VARIATIONS	• A group member can take the leader's part. • Other portable instruments such as bells or hand chimes can be used. • Participants can clap their hands and/or sing as the leader walks around the group.

3 *Where are the bells?*

PRINCIPAL AIM   To develop listening skills.

FURTHER AIMS   • To encourage group co-operation.
                • To develop patience and concentration.

EQUIPMENT   One pair of bells.

NUMBERS   4 to 8.

BASIC MODEL   The group sits in a circle, closely together. All participants put their hands behind their backs and then sing a song (e.g. 'Obladi-oblada') whilst passing the bells around behind their backs. When the song is finished the bells are held very still and group members (apart from the person holding the bells) are asked one after another to guess where the bells are.

OBSERVATIONS   • Participants should remain very quiet and still when the song has finished.
                • They may need reminding to keep their hands behind their backs during this activity.
                • Staff members can deliberately confuse participants by passing on imaginary bells.

VARIATIONS   • The direction in which the bells are passed around can be changed.
              • Two pairs of bells may be used.
              • The activity can be tried with closed eyes.

4 Time bomb

PRINCIPAL AIM   To develop the ability to listen to and to locate a sound source.

FURTHER AIMS
- To increase concentration.
- To develop group co-operation.

EQUIPMENT   Kitchen timer, clock or metronome.

NUMBERS   3 to 10.

BASIC MODEL   One of the group volunteers to leave the room. Another participant is asked to hide the timer. When this has been done, the volunteer is asked back into the room to listen to the timer and seek it out.

OBSERVATIONS
- The group may need encouragement to watch in silence without helping the seeker.

VARIATIONS
- The seeker can be blindfolded.
- An element of competition can be introduced by having seekers hunting simultaneously.
- The whole group can be invited to locate the sound. In this case, participants should move around the room quietly.
- The kitchen timer can be set for one or two minutes. The seeker must try to locate the timer before the bell rings.

5 Peace-lovers and warriors

PRINCIPAL AIM   To develop concentration and listening skills.

FURTHER AIMS
- To encourage group co-operation.
- To encourage group interaction.
- To develop auditory discrimination.
- To release energy.

EQUIPMENT   An instrument for each participant.

NUMBERS   6 to 10.

BASIC MODEL
- Participants choose either a quiet or a loud instrument. The group divides into two 'tribes': the quiet tribe (peace-lovers) and the loud tribe (warriors). The two tribes pretend to be on opposite banks of a wide river and communicate to each other as a group, playing in turns. Each tribe should listen when the other is playing.

OBSERVATIONS
- The peace-lovers should play very quietly, either not all playing at once or making use of silence.
- The two tribes should be encouraged to listen to one another and may be influenced by each other's playing.

VARIATIONS
- Each tribe can have a 'chief' who distributes the instruments and signals to the tribe when the playing should stop and start.
- Gentle or energetic dances can accompany the playing.

6 Quiet and loud

PRINCIPAL AIM — To develop patience and listening skills.

FURTHER AIMS —
- To develop anticipation skills.
- To increase concentration.

EQUIPMENT — An equal number of bells and tambourines so that each group member has one instrument. A keyboard or recorded music.

NUMBERS — 6 to 10.

BASIC MODEL — The two instrument groups sit facing each other ready to play in turn. The leader explains that those with bells play with the quiet music and those with tambourines play with the loud music. The music begins and the groups play accordingly.

OBSERVATIONS —
- A 'leader' or 'conductor' for each group may help in this activity.
- It may be useful, at first, to have a gap in between the two styles of music.
- Some participants may need encouragement to wait and listen while the other group is playing.

VARIATIONS —
- Two contrasting styles of music (e.g. lively and calm) can be used.
- A song or 'theme tune' may be repeated for each group; for example, 'Yellow Submarine' for the tambourine group and 'Are you going to Scarborough Fair?' for the bell group.

7 *Back to back*

PRINCIPAL AIM   To develop listening skills.

FURTHER AIMS
- To develop ability to take turns.
- To develop self-confidence.
- To encourage group co-operation.

EQUIPMENT   Two contrasting instruments.

NUMBERS   6 to 10.

BASIC MODEL   Participants are seated in a circle around two chairs placed back to back. Two volunteers are asked to sit on the chairs in the middle. They each select a different instrument and are asked to have a musical conversation, each playing in turn. At the end of their dialogue two other participants take their place.

OBSERVATIONS
- The two participants should not play for too long each time.
- The participants should try to explore the instruments and vary the dynamics.
- The leader may need to encourage the one who is not playing to listen rather than turn around and look.
- The participants who are not playing should listen and not interfere with the dialogue in the middle of the circle.

VARIATIONS
- The two players can imitate or echo one another.
- Two identical instruments can be used to encourage greater concentration.
- The two players can be blindfolded to enhance listening.
- The leader can ask the two players to determine a musical ending to their dialogue.

8 Contrary motion

PRINCIPAL AIM To develop listening skills and concentration.

FURTHER AIMS
- To encourage co-operation.
- To increase self-confidence.
- To encourage creativity.

EQUIPMENT Two small instruments. A keyboard or recorded music.

NUMBERS 6 to 10.

BASIC MODEL The group sits in a circle and the two instruments are given to two people sitting next to one another. When the music begins they pass the instruments round in opposite directions. When the music stops the group members holding the instruments play together. When the duet is over the music starts up again and the instruments are passed on in the same directions as before.

OBSERVATIONS
- A different piece of music may be played to accompany the players during their duet.
- If participants find it difficult to pass instruments round without playing them, beaters can be passed round instead. These can then be used on percussion instruments during the duets.

VARIATIONS
- The instruments can be passed round in the same direction. With a large group, three or four instruments can be used simultaneously.
- The difference between the passing round of the instruments and the playing of duets can be emphasized — the two participants about to play a duet change places (with their instruments) before starting to play.

9 Bells and tambourines

PRINCIPAL AIM   To develop concentration and group co-operation.

FURTHER AIMS
- To develop observational skills.
- To develop listening skills.

EQUIPMENT   An equal number of bells or tambourines so that each group member has one instrument. A keyboard or recorded music.

NUMBERS   6 to 10.

BASIC MODEL   Half the group has bells and the other half has tambourines. When the music starts, everyone dances around the room freely, playing the instruments. When the music stops, all the people with bells form one group and all the people with tambourines form another. When the music starts, everyone intermingles and dances freely again. The activity continues in this way.

OBSERVATIONS
- Initially, it may be helpful for a member of staff to join each group in order to help people gather together appropriately.

VARIATIONS
- Different portable instruments can be used.
- The activity can be made more challenging by using three different sets of instruments rather than two.
- Different types of instruments can be used. For example, wooden instruments such as woodblocks, claves and castanets for one group, and 'skin' instruments such as tambourines, tambours and small bongo drums for the other group.
- Different types of dance music may be explored.
- Once the bell group and the tambourine group have formed, each group can perform a short dance in turn before dispersing again.

10 Musical lines

PRINCIPAL AIM   To develop listening skills together with eye–hand co-ordination.

FURTHER AIMS   To develop pre-writing skills.

EQUIPMENT   A blackboard and chalk. Alternatively, a pen or pencil and a large piece of blank paper attached to the wall.

NUMBERS   3 to 8.

BASIC MODEL   One participant is at the blackboard, another is the 'singer'. The singer makes a clear vocal sound. The person at the blackboard immediately starts drawing a horizontal line. When the singer stops, the person drawing stops and leaves a large or small gap depending on the length of the silence before the singer starts singing again.

OBSERVATIONS   • In this activity either the singer or the drawer can lead.

VARIATIONS   • The leader can invite the whole group to sing, if the drawer leads.
    • The drawer can choose to draw a straight line (to correspond with a vocal sound on one pitch) or a line that goes up and down (to correspond with a vocal sound going up or down in pitch).
    • Instruments can be used instead of the voice. In this case different coloured pens can be used to identify the different instruments.
    • Participants can draw thick or thin lines, depending on how loud the sounds are.
    • Various group members can 'record' the same sound simultaneously on different pieces of paper. The group can then compare results.

11 Sound effects

PRINCIPAL AIM	To develop listening skills.
FURTHER AIMS	• To develop patience. • To develop imagination. • To increase group co-operation. • To prepare a group for an outing or to help a group remember a shared event.
EQUIPMENT	An instrument for each participant.
NUMBERS	4 to 10.
BASIC MODEL	The group sits in a circle. The leader chooses a topic, such as a future outing to a castle or a fire station. Each participant then chooses a word relating to the topic and an instrument to go with that word. The recorder may be chosen for the word 'wind', the castanets for 'footsteps', the duck-call for 'duck', etc. The leader then makes up a story relating to the chosen topic and every time the keywords are used in the narrative, participants play their instruments briefly.

OBSERVATIONS	• The leader can introduce this activity by encouraging participants to keep very quiet and listen to the sounds in the room or outside. • Participants may need encouragement to stop playing when their turn is over. It may help to ask them to put their instruments down after a few seconds. • The leader can use this activity to alleviate apprehension about a future outing. • The leader can repeat a keyword to keep the attention of a particular participant.
VARIATIONS	• Two participants can 'share' a keyword and play the same instrument. • A participant can determine all the keywords and distribute all the instruments. • Participants can make vocal sound effects instead of using instruments. • One participant can play all the sound effects as a solo. • Some participants can listen to the sounds without looking, instead of playing. They can then identify the corresponding words.

12 Motor-biking

PRINCIPAL AIM   To develop listening skills.

FURTHER AIMS
- To develop motor co-ordination and to speed up reactions.
- To provide an opportunity for energy release.
- To develop spatial awareness.
- To encourage creative vocalization.

EQUIPMENT   One kazoo.

NUMBERS   3 to 10.

BASIC MODEL   The group sits at one end of the room leaving sufficient space to run around. One participant chooses to be the motor-cyclist and prepares to ride an imaginary motor-bike around the room. The leader, or another participant, uses the kazoo to make the different sounds of the motor-bike, such as kick-starting, accelerating, slowing down and ticking over. The motor-cyclist has to listen to the different sounds as he or she 'rides' the motor-bike and must operate the bike accordingly.

OBSERVATIONS
- It may be helpful to explore different motor-bike sounds before 'starting' the motor-bike.
- This activity can stimulate a number of ideas relating to road safety.

VARIATIONS
- The leader can place chairs in the room to provide 'roundabouts', etc.
- Two participants can ride motor-bikes simultaneously, to the same kazoo cues.

13 Pied piper

PRINCIPAL AIM   To develop concentration and listening.

FURTHER AIMS   To develop a sense of trust.

EQUIPMENT   One mouth organ, one blindfold.

NUMBERS   3 to 6.

BASIC MODEL   Two participants stand facing each other. One (a volunteer) is blindfolded and asked to listen carefully to the other playing the mouth organ. The second participant walks slowly backwards whilst playing. The blindfolded person walks towards the sound and follows it around the room, without touching the player. When the player stops the music, both participants stand still.

OBSERVATIONS
- The instrumentalist should be encouraged to walk backwards slowly, not too far away from the blindfolded participant.
- It may be helpful to carry out this activity once without a blindfold.
- A member of staff can provide a model by being the first to be blindfolded.

VARIATIONS
- Furniture such as chairs can be placed around the room to form obstacles.
- Other group members can form obstacles by standing, lying or sitting around the room.
- Other small portable instruments can be used.
- Two pairs can operate at the same time using contrasting instruments.
- Two people can be blindfolded and walk together, holding hands.

14 Which way?

PRINCIPAL AIM	To develop listening and concentration.
FURTHER AIMS	• To develop group awareness.
	• To develop a sense of direction.
	• To encourage patience.
EQUIPMENT	One pair of bells and a keyboard.
NUMBERS	4 to 10.
BASIC MODEL	The group sits in a circle. When the music starts (in the middle range of the keyboard), group members pass the bells around the circle in a clockwise direction. Suddenly, the leader plays two high notes at the top of the keyboard and group members must then pass the bells around the circle in an anticlockwise direction. The music continues and every time the two high notes sound, the bells must change direction.

OBSERVATIONS	• The keyboard player need not be an experienced player. However, he or she should make sure the bells have changed direction correctly and have been passed on before playing the two high notes again.
	• Various group members can lead by playing the keyboard.
	• Participants may need encouragement to listen to the music rather than watch the player's hands move up and down the keyboard.
VARIATIONS	• Other small instruments such as maracas and cabasas can be passed around the circle.
	• Melodic instruments such as a large resonant xylophone can replace the keyboard.
	• The change of direction can be signalled by a beat on the cymbal or the drum. In this case, recorded music can replace the keyboard.

15 Listen, dance and paint!

PRINCIPAL AIM To develop listening skills and the ability to discriminate between different styles of music.

FURTHER AIMS
- To increase concentration.
- To develop the ability to relate sound to movement.
- To develop motor control.

EQUIPMENT Several large pieces of blank paper attached to walls or easels. Pots of paint and large paint brushes. A keyboard or contrasting pieces of recorded music: one fast and rhythmical, the other flowing and gentle.

NUMBERS 3 or 4.

BASIC MODEL The group dances to two contrasting pieces of music. Marching, stamping, clapping and jerky movements should be encouraged during the fast, rhythmical piece of music and slow, turning and fluid movements should be encouraged during the flowing, gentle piece of music. Participants then paint on the large pieces of paper while listening to the two pieces of music again. The paintings can then be discussed and the contrasting styles of music may be evident in the different styles of painting.

OBSERVATIONS
- Each person will move or paint in an individual manner and there is no 'correct' way to perform to certain types of music. The leader should encourage participants to explore rather than teach them set ways of dancing or painting.

VARIATIONS
- Contrasting colours of paint (bright and dull) or textures (thick and thin) can be used.
- Thick felt pens can be used instead of paints.
- During the painting, the leader can stop the music and ask each participant to move on to the next participant's painting. Painting continues when the music starts again. Participants may either leave colours at each painting or carry them around from painting to painting.

16 Listen and remember!

PRINCIPAL AIM   To develop the ability to remember past events.

FURTHER AIMS
- To develop the ability to empathize with other participants.
- To develop listening skills and imagination.

EQUIPMENT   Bongo drums.

NUMBERS   3 to 10.

BASIC MODEL   The group sits in a circle. The leader asks the group to remember a special occasion such as an outing or a holiday. One participant thinks about an event during the special occasion and attempts to play the bongo drums in a way which will remind other participants of this event. After playing for a short time, he or she puts the bongo drums down and participants are invited to guess which event the player was thinking about. Another participant then takes over the bongo drums and the activity continues.

OBSERVATIONS
- Participants may need encouragement to wait until the player has finished playing and put the bongo drums down before making suggestions.
- Participants may need encouragement to listen to the playing and link the sound to the specific event rather than simply guess at random what the player is thinking about.
- It may be necessary for the player to ask individual participants for suggestions rather than let everyone guess at once.

VARIATIONS
- Other instruments can be used. Each participant could choose a different instrument. Some may wish to play several instruments.
- The group can talk about the special occasion and write down a series of events that occurred, using small pieces of paper. These can be randomly distributed to participants who each then play about their particular event.
- Other shared events such as a cookery session or play time can be remembered.

17 Hunt the sweet!

PRINCIPAL AIM   To develop concentration and listening skills.

FURTHER AIMS   To encourage group co-operation.

EQUIPMENT   A few sweets.

NUMBERS   4 to 6.

BASIC MODEL   One volunteer is asked to leave the room. The leader then hides a sweet. The volunteer is invited back into the room to search for the sweet. The group assists him or her by clapping loudly and quietly. The nearer he or she gets to the sweet, the quieter the clapping becomes. When the clapping stops, the sweet should be within reach.

OBSERVATIONS   • The seeker should be encouraged to notice how his or her position in the room affects the volume of sound. If necessary, he or she can return to the door and begin again.
   • The group should be encouraged to watch the distance between the seeker and the sweet, and monitor the sound level accordingly.

VARIATIONS   • Vocal 'oo' sounds can be used instead of clapping.
   • Instruments can be used instead of clapping.
   • Recorded music can be used and one participant asked to control the volume level.
   • The 'seeker' can be guided by one group member (playing an instrument or clapping) instead of by the whole group.
   • A small instrument such as bells can be hidden instead of sweets.

18 Catch a rhythm!

PRINCIPAL AIM To develop listening skills.

FURTHER AIMS
- To increase concentration.
- To develop short-term memory.

EQUIPMENT None.

NUMBERS 3 to 8.

BASIC MODEL The group sits in a circle. The leader claps a simple rhythm which can easily be repeated continuously (e.g. ♩ ♩ ♩). When participants feel able, they join in until the whole group is clapping together. The leader may then stop the group and clap a different rhythm.

OBSERVATIONS
- Participants may need encouragement to listen carefully rather than clap at random.

VARIATIONS
- The rhythms can be tapped on different parts of the body.
- Words can be used to accompany the rhythm. For example, 'Da-vid Hall' or 'Plums and cus-tard'.
- Group members can be asked to lead.
- Taped music can be used as a support.
- Instruments such as tambours or tambourines can be used.
- The group can 'echo' back short rhythms.
- Participants can repeat the given rhythm one after another, in turn.
- When one rhythm has been established the leader can change to a different one without a break. He or she can call 'All change' to alert the group to the new rhythm.

19 Big Ben

PRINCIPAL AIM   To develop patience.

FURTHER AIMS
- To develop motor control.
- To develop eye–hand co-ordination.
- To encourage listening.
- To develop group co-operation.

EQUIPMENT   D, G, A and B chime bars.

NUMBERS   5 to 10.

BASIC MODEL   Four participants have a chime bar each and stand side by side facing the other group members. The chime bars are arranged in sequence of pitch D, G, A and B from left to right. The leader acts as a conductor and indicates to each player when he or she should play in order to make up 'Big Ben's' chime.

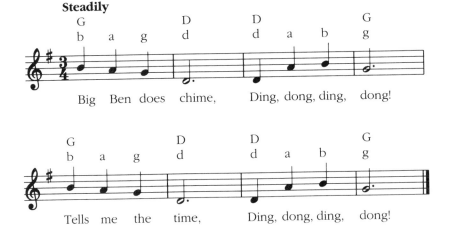

OBSERVATIONS
- The group leader should be familiar with the tune beforehand, especially the second and fourth phrases, in order to direct the players correctly.
- It may be helpful for the whole group to sing the 'Big Ben' melody first in order to become acquainted with the tune.

VARIATIONS
- One of the participants can chime a particular time after the tune has been played.
- The four players can play without a leader once they are familiar with the tune.
- Hand-chimes can be used instead of chime bars.
- The four players can experiment with different four-note phrases.
- One participant can play the chime bars held by four others. In this case the four holding the chime bars should put their sticks down.

24

20 Mystery notes

PRINCIPAL AIM   To develop concentration.

FURTHER AIMS
- To develop observational skills.
- To develop auditory memory.
- To encourage group co-operation.

EQUIPMENT   One metallophone and a beater.

NUMBERS   3 to 10.

BASIC MODEL   The group sits in a circle. One participant plays two notes on a metallophone. He or she then passes the instrument to another player who repeats the same two notes. The second player plays his or her two notes before passing the instrument on again, etc. If a participant cannot remember which two notes have been played, the two notes can either be repeated or the group can be asked to assist.

OBSERVATIONS
- Staff may help by playing two easy notes (e.g. the top and bottom notes of the instrument) for participants who find this activity difficult.
- Several notes can be taken off the metallophone to make this activity easier.

VARIATIONS
- Instead of two notes, one or three notes can be played.
- Three instruments can be placed in the middle of the circle and participants play two of the three instruments each time.
- The number of different notes rather than the exact pitches of the notes can be repeated. Up to five notes can be played and the correct number of notes repeated. This variation can also be played on untuned instruments such as the bongos or the tambourine.

21 Ding or dong

PRINCIPAL AIM To increase concentration.

FURTHER AIMS
- To develop auditory discrimination.
- To speed up reactions.
- To encourage group co-operation.

EQUIPMENT   None.

NUMBERS   6 to 10.

BASIC MODEL   The group sits in a circle. The leader explains that a sound will be passed around the circle. The word 'ding' will make the sound go to the left, and the word 'dong' will make the sound go to the right. For example, players A, B, and C are sitting next to each other. A says 'ding'. His or her left-hand neighbour B answers 'ding'. C, who is sitting on the left of B, answers 'dong'. B will then say 'ding' if he or she wants the sound to go to C, and 'dong' if the sound is to go to A. The activity continues around the circle in this way.

OBSERVATIONS
- It may be helpful to establish the direction of each sound by suggesting that the group 'pass' the two sounds around the groups separately once or twice before the activity is started.

VARIATIONS
- Instead of using the words 'ding' and 'dong', group members can tap their left and right knees to indicate the direction of sound.
- Small instruments held by group members can be used as a substitute for 'ding' and/or 'dong'. If two instruments are used to indicate directions, instruments that can be played in one hand should be chosen. The instruments should be clearly held in left or right hands depending on which direction they indicate.
- Percussion instruments can be played once to make the sound go left and twice to make the sound go right.

II Activities to develop a sense of self and awareness of others

Scarecrow

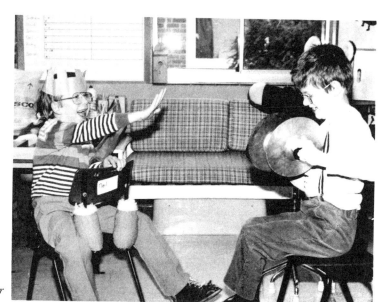

Conductor

22 Hello!

PRINCIPAL AIM   To develop individual awareness within a group setting.

FURTHER AIMS
- To develop eye contact.
- To develop awareness of different group members and their names.
- To develop patience.

EQUIPMENT   One guiro or one maraca.

NUMBERS   3 to 8.

BASIC MODEL   Participants sit in a circle with the leader in the middle. The leader uses the guiro to play, say or sing 'hello' to each person individually, using their name. The aim is to stimulate the greeted person to reciprocate some form of 'hello' to the guiro.

OBSERVATIONS
- The guiro is particularly useful because the sound is easily controlled.
- Those not being greeted should be encouraged to listen. If listeners become restless, they can be asked to tell the leader who should be greeted next, or to remind the group who still remains to be greeted.
- Paper eyes can be stuck on the instruments.

VARIATIONS
- A non-verbal participant can be offered a stick to stroke the guiro in reply to the 'hello'.
- A group member can become the leader.
- Different instruments can be used.
- A puppet, doll or stuffed animal can be used to greet each group member.

23 *Pop! goes the instrument*

PRINCIPAL AIM   To encourage people to make choices.

FURTHER AIMS   • To develop patience.
                 • To improve concentration.

EQUIPMENT   A large box containing at least as many instruments as there are participants.

NUMBERS   3 to 10.

BASIC MODEL   Participants sit in a semicircle facing the box. This should be placed high enough so that participants are unable to see the instruments inside. The leader sings 'Half a pound of tuppenny rice'. On the word 'Pop!' he or she pulls one instrument emphatically out of the box and holds it up. The person who shows the most immediate interest is given the instrument, encouraged to play it briefly, then place it on the floor near his or her chair. The activity continues until as many instruments as are required are distributed. This should then lead on to another activity where participants all play instruments together.

OBSERVATIONS   • Changing the pace and emphasis of the song each time can sustain the attention of participants.
                 • Participants can join in with the singing.

VARIATIONS   • Instruments can be brought out from behind a screen or a piano.
                 • Participants can name the instruments before they are distributed.
                 • Two instruments can be distributed at once.

24 *Listen and choose!*

PRINCIPAL AIM
- To develop initiative and encourage sharing.

FURTHER AIMS
- To develop auditory discrimination.
- To develop confidence to make a choice in a group situation.
- To develop tolerance.

EQUIPMENT
An instrument for each group participant. A suitable screen behind which to hide the instruments, such as a large piece of furniture or a piano.

NUMBERS
3 to 10.

BASIC MODEL
The instruments are all hidden behind the screen. The leader plays one instrument, and the person who shows the most interest (or who can name the instrument) is given it to play. This is done with all the instruments until each person has an instrument. Once everyone has an instrument the group plays together.

OBSERVATIONS
- Some participants may wish to name hidden instruments while others may show their preference simply by smiling.
- Instruments may be played briefly by participants after they have received them.
- It may minimize distractions if the leader encourages participants to place their instruments on their laps or on the floor until they have all received their instruments.

VARIATIONS
- A group member can take the leader's role behind the screen.
- Two instruments can be played simultaneously.
- Participants can choose an instrument to give to another person.
- Participants can comment on their choices of instruments or people.

25 Solo time

PRINCIPAL AIM   To increase self-confidence.

FURTHER AIMS   • To develop patience.
                • To encourage group co-operation and understanding.

EQUIPMENT   One maraca.

NUMBERS   3 to 8.

BASIC MODEL   The maraca is passed around the group whilst a short song (e.g. 'London Bridge is falling down') or part of a song is sung. When the song is finished, the participant holding the instrument plays a free solo. After the solo, the song starts up again, the instrument is passed around and the activity continues.

OBSERVATIONS
• The group leader may have to ensure that each participant is given the opportunity to play a solo.
• A clear distinction should be made between solo time and passing the instrument around the circle.
• The leader may need to encourage participants to listen carefully to the soloist.

VARIATIONS
• The song can be sung quickly or slowly. The speed will probably affect the way in which the instrument is passed around.
• Different songs can be used.
• Players may wish to stand for their solo.
• Each soloist can say or sing his or her name before or during the playing.
• Two instruments can be passed around, travelling either in the same way or in opposite directions. The soloists can then play a duet or two solos, one after another.
• The 'listeners' can clap hands while the soloist is playing.
• Different instruments can be passed around.
• Instead of singing a song and then having solos, participants can take it in turns to play a solo one after another. The player should pass the instrument on to the next soloist after he or she has finished playing.
• Soloists can play about their own feelings or about another group member's feelings. Other group members can guess what those feelings are and who is being played about.

26 Twirling tambourine

PRINCIPAL AIM   To motivate people to take the initiative.

FURTHER AIMS   • To develop patience.
                • To develop self-control.

EQUIPMENT   One tambourine or tambour.

NUMBERS   3 to 6.

BASIC MODEL   The group sits in a circle. The group leader stands in front of one of the participants, holding a tambourine vertically. The participant is invited to tap the tambourine once. In response to the way it is tapped, the leader twirls around on the spot. If the tambourine is tapped lightly, the leader only goes part of the way around and then swings back to his or her original position. If the tambourine is tapped loudly, the leader twirls right around. Another group member is then invited to take a turn at tapping.

OBSERVATIONS   • Group members may need help to tap the tambourine once only for each twirl.

VARIATIONS   • The tambourine can be held at different heights and angles.
              • A participant can take the leading role and become the person who twirls with the tambourine.

27 Moving mouse

PRINCIPAL AIM   To develop tactile awareness.

FURTHER AIMS
- To develop tolerance of physical contact.
- To develop awareness of different body parts.
- To develop listening and concentration.
- To develop patience.
- To develop a sense of trust.

EQUIPMENT   One toy mouse or puppet, a tambourine and a blindfold.

NUMBERS   3 to 6.

BASIC MODEL   Two participants sit on chairs facing one another. One is blindfolded and the other has the tambourine. The leader stands close to the blindfolded person and has the mouse. The other participants should watch quietly. As the tambourine is played, the leader makes the mouse move continuously on the blindfolded person. When the tambourine stops, the mouse stops. The mouse moves around in different ways (e.g. jumps, creeps, runs or crawls) depending on whether the tambourine is played loudly or quietly, fast or slowly. After a while, other participants are blindfolded and/or play the tambourine.

OBSERVATIONS
- The blindfolded person must keep his or her hands still and feel the mouse rather than catch it with his or her hands.
- Participants can talk about how it feels having the mouse moving around on them.
- For some sensitive participants, it may be necessary to move the mouse in a firm and definite manner and perhaps begin without using the blindfold.

VARIATIONS
- A group member can operate the mouse.
- Other instruments or toy animals/puppets can be used.
- Two different instruments can be used: one to make the mouse run, for example; another to make the mouse jump.
- Different instruments can be used to make the mouse move to different parts of the body. For example, bells for the arms, drum for the legs.
- Instead of playing the tambourine, the person operating the mouse can improvise a song describing the mouse's movements.

28 *Where shall I play?*

PRINCIPAL AIM To develop initiative.

FURTHER AIMS
- To develop listening skills.
- To encourage group co-operation.

EQUIPMENT A tambourine for each group member. A keyboard or recorded dance music.

NUMBERS 3 to 10.

BASIC MODEL Group members play their tambourines and dance freely to the music. After a few minutes, the group leader lowers the volume of the music and suggests that participants play their tambourines in a variety of different places such as behind backs, on the wall, on the floor, on knees, on another group member's back, etc.

OBSERVATIONS
- Quiet gentle music encourages group members not to be too energetic when playing on each other.

VARIATIONS
- Group members can suggest various places to play the tambourines.
- Participants can balance their tambourines on various parts of their bodies, such as heads or arms.
- Group members can get into pairs and share a tambourine for all these activities.

29 Scarecrow

PRINCIPAL AIM	To develop group co-operation.
FURTHER AIMS	• To develop patience; to improve motor control; to increase self-confidence.
EQUIPMENT	Small pieces of different-coloured material, each about 20cm square, one for each participant.
NUMBERS	3 to 10.
BASIC MODEL	The group sits in a circle. Each participant chooses one piece of material. One person goes to the middle of the circle and stands still with arms stretched out to the sides. Each participant goes to the middle of the circle and puts his or her piece of material on the first person's head, arms, shoulders or feet. The group then sits down again (except for the 'scarecrow' in the middle) and sings a slow song such as a version of 'She's a lassie from Lancashire' (see tune below). The scarecrow in the middle moves slowly and carefully, making sure that no pieces of material fall off. The song progressively speeds up and the scarecrow finally shakes off all the pieces of material.

(Tune: *She's a lassie from Lancashire*)

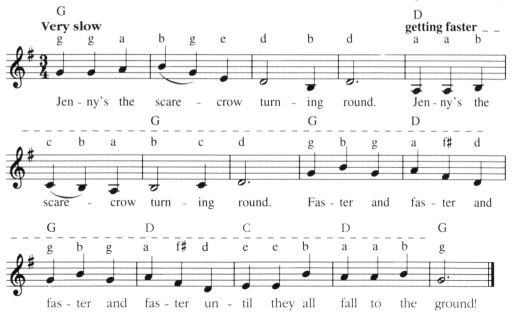

OBSERVATIONS	• The singing can be accompanied by clapping, and the scarecrow rewarded by a round of applause once all the pieces of material have been shaken off. • The scarecrow may need help at the beginning in order to stay still.
VARIATIONS	• Two or three participants can be scarecrows together and can hold hands when they start moving. • This activity follows on well from 'Shake it off!' (p. 70) which gives all the group participants an opportunity to 'shake' together.

30 *Growing flowers*

PRINCIPAL AIM To develop awareness of leadership and increase self-confidence.

FURTHER AIMS
- To motivate group members to take part actively.
- To develop observational skills.

EQUIPMENT An instrument for each person, two or three large cardboard flowers on sticks.

NUMBERS 3 or 4.

BASIC MODEL One group member plays an instrument while the others listen. Gradually, as the instrument is played, a flower (held on a long stick by a hidden member of staff) appears from behind the piano or another large piece of furniture. If the player stops playing, the flower stops growing. If the playing is fast and loud, the flower grows more quickly. Once the flower can grow no further, it can be made either to dance or to wither slowly, depending on the style of the music played.

OBSERVATIONS
- If possible, the room used should have a high ceiling so that flowers can grow sufficiently.

VARIATIONS
- Two people, each with a different instrument, can play at the same time, making two flowers grow.
- A group member can help move the flowers.
- Different colours or types of flowers can be used to provide variety.

31 Name game

PRINCIPAL AIM	To encourage vocalization.
FURTHER AIMS	• To develop leadership skills. • To develop listening. • To encourage group co-operation.
EQUIPMENT	None.
NUMBERS	4 to 10.
BASIC MODEL	The group sits in a circle. The leader calls out a participant's name in a

rhythmic manner (e.g. Timothy Timothy). The group joins in with the chant until the leader signals to stop. Another name is repeated in a contrasting

rhythm (e.g. Sarah Sarah). After three names have been called, the leader divides the group into three subgroups, one for each name. The leader then conducts, asking each subgroup to start and stop, chant loudly or quietly, fast or slowly. The name groups can chant separately or simultaneously. The activity then continues with new names and a new leader.

OBSERVATIONS	• The rhythms of names can be used very freely and the same name used in

very different ways, e.g. Jim--my Jim--my or JimmyJimmyJimmyJimmy.
• It may help to vary the pitches for different syllables.

VARIATIONS	• Names of foods, toys, furniture or animals can be used. • Nonsense sounds such as 'whaoh', 'rumdidledoo' or 'pip' can be used. • Words can be accompanied by clapping.

32 *Circle the drum!*

PRINCIPAL AIM   To develop self-confidence.

FURTHER AIMS
- To develop group co-operation.
- To develop initiative.
- To increase concentration.
- To develop listening skills.

EQUIPMENT   One drum and two beaters.

NUMBERS   4 to 8.

BASIC MODEL   The group sits on the floor around the drum and the beaters. The leader walks around the group and sings a song (e.g. 'What shall we do with the drunken sailor?' or 'English country garden'). When the song ends, the leader stops behind a group member who then stands up to play a drum solo. Other group members can clap to accompany the solo. When the playing is over, the drummer puts down the beaters, tags on to the leader and walks around the group with the leader. This continues until all group members have played a solo and formed a long line behind the leader.

OBSERVATIONS
- Every time the leader stops behind a group member, he or she can ask the group who it is. This helps participants to concentrate and prepares the soloist for his or her solo.
- Different group members will probably play for varying lengths of time. The group leader may need to help a participant stop by saying, 'One, two, three . . . Stop!'.

VARIATIONS
- A different instrument, such as a cymbal or a metallophone, can be used.
- The leader can stop between two people rather than behind one person. The two people on either side of the leader can then have a duet.
- A variety of songs can be used for this activity.
- A group participant can act as leader.

33 Conductor

PRINCIPAL AIM	To develop leadership skills.
FURTHER AIMS	• To explore non-verbal communication. • To develop eye contact. • To develop self-confidence.
EQUIPMENT	Three contrasting instruments.
NUMBERS	4 to 10.
BASIC MODEL	Three participants are players, a fourth acts as conductor. Other group members participate as an audience. The conductor first establishes clear hand signals for starting and stopping (e.g. pointing for starting and a raised hand for stopping). He or she then encourages the participants to play according to the hand signals. Players can play one at a time or together. New participants can take over as conductor and players when the first group has finished playing.

OBSERVATIONS	• The conductor can make use of silence between different instrumental entries. • No directions should be verbal. • If the conductor stands on a chair, this may help him or her to lead and encourages the players to sustain eye contact rather than look at their instruments.
VARIATIONS	• Other signals can be established for loud and soft, fast and slow, etc. • Vocal sounds can be substituted for instruments. • The whole group (apart from the conductor) can play instruments either individually or in subgroups. For example, a drum section, a wind section and a bell section. • The conductor can use a 'conducting' stick and/or white gloves. • The instruments can be placed on different coloured mats and the conductor can hold up samples of these colours to indicate which instrument should be played. • The conductor can hold up pictures of the instruments he or she wishes to hear.

34 Clap and tap!

PRINCIPAL AIM | To develop initiative.

FURTHER AIMS
- To speed up reactions.
- To develop listening and observational skills.
- To encourage group co-operation.

EQUIPMENT | One tambour or tambourine.

NUMBERS | 4 to 8.

BASIC MODEL | The group sits in a circle, either on chairs or on the floor. Participants should be as quiet as possible before starting. The group leader is in the middle of the circle and suggests that one person should clap once. As soon as the clap is heard, the leader holds out the tambour to the person who has clapped and that person then taps the tambour, once. Another participant claps and the leader holds out the tambour for that person, and so on.

OBSERVATIONS
- Some participants may need encouragement to clap and thereby 'request' the tambour; others may need to curb their enthusiasm and concentrate on listening and watching other group members take part.

VARIATIONS
- A group member can become the leader.

35 Come and get it!

PRINCIPAL AIM   To develop eye contact.

FURTHER AIMS
- To develop initiative.
- To develop listening skills.
- To encourage mobility.

EQUIPMENT   One pair of Indian cymbals (or another quiet instrument).

NUMBERS   4 to 8.

BASIC MODEL   The group sits in a circle, with one person holding the Indian cymbals. When all is quiet, that person plays the cymbals, looking directly at a second group member. When he or she has finished playing, the second person gets up, takes the cymbals from the player and returns to his or her chair. The activity then continues.

OBSERVATIONS
- Eye contact is assured by the person getting up to fetch the instrument. This would not be the case if the player pointed to another player or if he or she gave the instrument away.
- People with limited mobility can acknowledge eye contact by a signal and can then be helped to collect the instrument.

VARIATIONS
- Two instruments can be used by different people at the same time.

36 Make up your dance!

PRINCIPAL AIM	To increase confidence in solo performance.
FURTHER AIMS	• To encourage creativity.
	• To develop patience and improve ability to listen.
EQUIPMENT	Approximately twenty pieces of different-coloured material, each about 20cm square. A keyboard or recorded dance music in various styles.
NUMBERS	3 to 6.
BASIC MODEL	One group member is the solo performer while the others form the audience. The soloist lays out the pieces of material in any way that he or she likes, chooses a fast or slow piece of music and then dances, using the pieces of material as stepping stones or as points to dance around. Once the dance is over, the audience claps and the soloist passes the pieces of material to another participant.

OBSERVATIONS	• If members of the audience get restless, they can join in by clapping.
	• Some performers may want to choose a specific piece of music to dance to rather than a slow or fast piece of music.
VARIATIONS	• The audience can accompany the dancer by playing instruments.
	• Two performers may want to dance together or a performer may choose to be accompanied by another group member playing a particular instrument.
	• Hoops can be used instead of pieces of material if a large room is available.
	• This activity follows on well from 'Dance with a glued foot!' (p. 86) where all participants dance at once.

37 Guess who!

PRINCIPAL AIM   To encourage empathy.

FURTHER AIMS
- To encourage awareness of others.
- To develop listening skills.
- To develop observational skills.

EQUIPMENT   An instrument for each participant.

NUMBERS   4 to 10.

BASIC MODEL   The group sits in a circle and each participant has an instrument. The leader encourages everyone to play together and listen carefully to each other. After a short time, the leader signals to the group to stop playing and put the instruments down. One participant then picks up his or her instrument and plays a short solo in such a way as to remind the rest of the group of another participant. Once the solo is over, the rest of the group has to guess who the soloist has been playing about. The activity continues with further solos about other participants.

OBSERVATIONS
- Participants should let the soloist finish playing and put the instrument down before guessing who the piece of music was about.
- It may be appropriate for participants to comment on the solos.
- With a large group, it may be helpful to intersperse the solos with group playing.

VARIATIONS
- Solos can also be about people who are known to the group but not present.
- Solos can be about pictures on the walls instead of about people.

38 *The empty chair*

PRINCIPAL AIM   To develop initiative.

FURTHER AIMS
- To develop listening skills.
- To develop eye contact and non-verbal communication.

EQUIPMENT   A portable instrument for each participant.

NUMBERS   6 to 10.

BASIC MODEL   The group sits in a circle which includes one vacant chair. Each participant has a portable instrument. The person with the vacant chair to their right tries, through eye contact and instrument playing, to entice another group member to come and sit next to him or her. The rest of the group listens while this dialogue is taking place. Once the empty chair has been filled, the person to the left of the newly vacant chair continues.

OBSERVATIONS
- The leader may need to encourage group members to listen to the person playing.
- Talking should be discouraged. All communication should be through instrument playing, eye contact and gesture.

VARIATIONS
- An instrument can be placed on the vacant chair and the person moving leaves his or her instrument behind.

III Activities to develop social skills

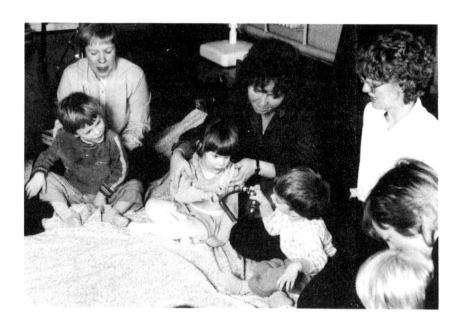

Kings and queens of the bells

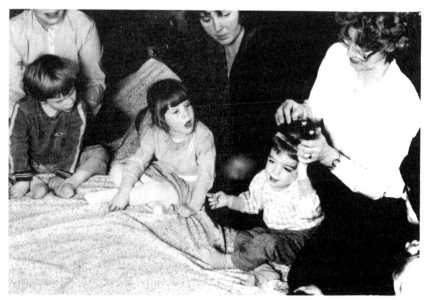

39 *Swaying hoops*

PRINCIPAL AIM To develop the ability to share.

FURTHER AIMS • To improve sitting balance and motor control.
• To develop listening skills.

EQUIPMENT Half as many hoops as there are participants. A keyboard or recorded 'swaying' music.

NUMBERS 4 to 10.

BASIC MODEL Participants sit on the floor in pairs, facing one another, and hold opposite sides of the hoops. When the music starts, each pair sways backwards and forwards, holding on to the hoop. When the music stops, everyone keeps still.

OBSERVATIONS • Sitting positions will vary and each participant should be encouraged to find a comfortable position.

VARIATIONS • The speed of the music and the swaying can be varied.
• Participants can sway from side to side instead of backwards and forwards.
• The hoops can be put aside to allow pairs to sway by holding hands (in a traditional 'Row, row, row your boat' fashion).

40 Make me dance!

PRINCIPAL AIM   To develop group awareness.

FURTHER AIMS
- To develop skills of anticipation.
- To develop observational skills.
- To develop self-confidence.

EQUIPMENT   One glove puppet.

NUMBERS   3 to 6.

BASIC MODEL   The group sits in a circle. The leader makes the puppet dance from one participant to another. The group sings a song (e.g. 'Shall we dance?') during this dance. When the song is finished, the person on whom the puppet has landed takes over and helps it to dance on his or her knee. When this 'individual' dance is over, the leader again makes the puppet dance from person to person.

OBSERVATIONS
- The leader can either make the puppet dance in an orderly way from one person to another around the circle, or in a random way across the circle.
- During the individual dance, the group can sing or clap to a different tune.

VARIATIONS
- A stuffed animal (e.g. a beanbag frog, a life-size teddy bear) can be used instead of the puppet.
- A group member can make the puppet dance around the room.
- If a stuffed animal is used, the group, rather than the group leader, can pass it round.

41 Sending messages

PRINCIPAL AIM	To develop the ability to take turns.
FURTHER AIMS	• To encourage eye contact. • To develop listening and concentration.
EQUIPMENT	Two contrasting instruments.
NUMBERS	4 to 10.
BASIC MODEL	The group sits in a circle. Two people sitting opposite one another each choose an instrument. One of the two begins by playing his or her instrument. The other person waits and listens, as do the rest of the group. When the first player has finished, he or she looks up at the second participant, who then begins to play. When the second player has finished, he or she looks up at the first player. When they have each taken sufficient turns and the dialogue is over, they pass on the instruments, clockwise, to the next two people, and the activity continues.

OBSERVATIONS	• It may be advisable for two members of staff to demonstrate this activity first.
VARIATIONS	• Listeners can comment on the players' music. • Players can imitate their partners' styles of playing (rhythm and/or dynamics). • Humming or vocal sounds can be used instead of instruments.

48

42 Humpty's downfall

PRINCIPAL AIM To develop skills of anticipation.

FURTHER AIMS
- To develop listening skills.
- To release energy.

EQUIPMENT An instrument for each group member.

NUMBERS 3 to 10.

BASIC MODEL The group sits in a circle. Each person has an instrument. The group sings the beginning of the song 'Humpty Dumpty' (see tune below). At the words '... had a great fall ...', everyone plays as loudly as possible. After a few moments of loud instrumental playing, there should be a brief silence and the rest of the song may then be sung quietly.

OBSERVATIONS
- The group may require direction if the leader wants a quiet, subsiding end to the song.

VARIATIONS
- The instruments can be left in the middle on the floor and the group can 'fall down' to play them.

43 Kings and queens of the bells

PRINCIPAL AIM	To develop group co-operation.
FURTHER AIMS	• To encourage listening. • To develop self-confidence. • To develop motor control.
EQUIPMENT	One pair of bells.
NUMBERS	4 to 10.
BASIC MODEL	The group sits in a circle. As group members pass the bells around the circle, the leader names each participant using the following song (or recitation): 'Julie pass the bells to Brian, Brian pass the bells to John, John pass the bells to Sylvia ... Sylvia pass them on to Ruth' (see tune below). At this point 'Ruth' holds on to the bells and balances them on her head. The group then claps hands energetically while singing or saying: 'Ruth's the queen of the bells today (×3) ... Clap your hands for Ruth, yeah!' The group then start passing the bells and singing once more.

OBSERVATIONS	• The leader should make a clear contrast between the slow, quiet passing of the bells and the energetic clapping. • If the words are said rather than sung, the leader should say them like a nursery rhyme with exaggerated stresses and pauses.
VARIATIONS	• Other small instruments can be used. In this case, instead of becoming kings or queens, participants can play solos while the group claps and says: 'Ruth has the tambourine, Ruth has the tambourine ...' etc.

44 All change!

PRINCIPAL AIM To develop group co-operation.

FURTHER AIMS
- To speed up reactions.
- To develop listening skills.

EQUIPMENT One small instrument for each person. A keyboard or recorded music.

NUMBERS 4 to 10.

BASIC MODEL The group sits in a circle and each participant has an instrument. The leader plays a piece of music and members of the group join in on their instruments. When the music stops, they place their instruments on the chairs and each person moves to the seat on his or her left. The activity starts up again when all participants are waiting, ready to play their 'new' instrument.

OBSERVATIONS
- It may be necessary to practise standing up and putting instruments down when the music stops before embarking on this activity.
- Participants may need help to keep quiet until the music begins again each time.

VARIATIONS
- Different types of music can be used during this activity.
- Participants can move to any chair they like rather than just to the chair on their left.
- If a keyboard is used, the person playing the keyboard can be included in the circle and move to the left when the music stops. This means that participants have a chance to 'lead' from the keyboard.

45 Farewell symphony

PRINCIPAL AIM   To develop self-control.

FURTHER AIMS
- To encourage group co-operation.
- To develop patience.

EQUIPMENT   An instrument for each person. A box for the instruments.

NUMBERS   5 to 10.

BASIC MODEL   The group sits in a circle around an empty box. Each person has an instrument. The leader plays a rhythm or tune and encourages everyone to join in. When the group has played together for a while, one player puts his or her instrument in the box. (The leader may need to arrange this beforehand.) The person to the left follows soon after, and so on until all the instruments are in the box.

OBSERVATIONS
- The leader may need to support the group through vocal sounds or clapping as members discard their instruments.
- The leader may need to prevent participants taking other instruments out of the box when they are putting their instruments away.
- The long diminuendo resulting from this activity can have a calming effect on the group, valuable at the end of the session.

VARIATIONS
- This activity can be used in reverse for distributing instruments.
- When an instrument has been put away the player can hum quietly. The humming can become quieter at the very end.
- The leader, or another group member, can use eye contact to direct participants to put their instruments away.

46 Dance and change!

PRINCIPAL AIM   To develop the ability to share.

FURTHER AIMS
- To develop initiative.
- To develop listening skills.

EQUIPMENT   A variety of small portable instruments, one for each participant. A keyboard or recorded dance music.

NUMBERS   4 to 10.

BASIC MODEL   Each participant chooses one small portable instrument. Dance music is played and everyone dances and plays an instrument simultaneously. When the music stops, participants exchange instruments. When the music starts again, everyone resumes dancing.

OBSERVATIONS
- If some participants find it hard to give up their instruments, it may help to start the music again as soon as most instruments have been exchanged.

VARIATIONS
- Participants can dance in pairs and share an instrument. In this case, partners and/or instruments can be exchanged when the music stops. Holding hands may help some pairs to stay together during the dancing. Couples can include clapping games or movement imitation in their dancing.
- Different types of dance music can be used, with participants moving and dancing in a variety of ways.
- Half the group only has instruments. When the music stops, the instrumentalists offer their instruments to participants who are without instruments.

47 Roll or throw!

PRINCIPAL AIM	To develop the ability to co-operate in a group situation.
FURTHER AIMS	• To develop auditory discrimination. • To develop eye contact. • To develop the ability to relate sound to movement.
EQUIPMENT	Two contrasting instruments. One ball.
NUMBERS	6 to 10.
BASIC MODEL	The group sits in a circle and one person is asked to sit outside the circle with two contrasting instruments. One of the participants in the circle has the ball. Participants decide which instrument should indicate that the ball be thrown, and which that it should be rolled. When the instrumentalist plays one instrument, the person with the ball rolls or throws it to another participant, according to what has been decided. The instrumentalist may pause while playing, in which case the ball should be held still.

OBSERVATIONS	• The leader may need to encourage the instrumentalist to pause in between playing each instrument. • The instrumentalist may face away from the group in order not to be distracted. • Participants may need encouragement to stay seated when rolling or throwing the ball.
VARIATIONS	• Two contrasting songs can be used by the instrumentalist. • Different types and sizes of balls can be used. • Other items such as bean bags and hoops (to slide along the floor) can be used. • Other ways of passing the ball, such as spinning or rolling with the foot, can be explored. Three or more instruments can be used.

48 *What now?*

PRINCIPAL AIM	To develop group co-operation.
FURTHER AIMS	• To develop the ability to make a choice and be decisive. • To develop the ability to remember past events.
EQUIPMENT	Blank cards or pieces of paper and writing material. A hat for the cards.
NUMBERS	3 to 10.
BASIC MODEL	The leader asks participants to remember musical activities they have taken part in as a group. They write these on cards and place them in a hat. The group leader or a participant selects one card and the group embarks on that activity.

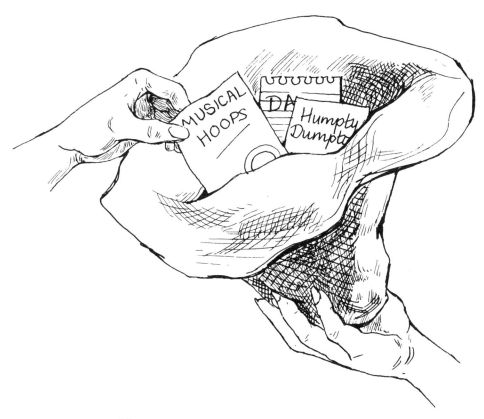

OBSERVATIONS	• This activity can be used at the beginning of a session. • It is particularly valuable for groups who have difficulty in decision-making. • With a small group, each participant can select an activity.
VARIATIONS	• Participants can draw pictures symbolizing activities instead of writing them down. • The group leader can suggest that participants remember either seated activities or activities involving movement.

49 Hat dance

PRINCIPAL AIM   To develop group co-operation.

FURTHER AIMS
- To increase concentration.
- To develop group awareness.
- To develop a sense of responsibility and caring.

EQUIPMENT   A hat. A keyboard or recorded music.

NUMBERS   4 to 8.

BASIC MODEL   The group sits in a circle. When the music begins, the hat is passed around the group, with each person in turn placing it on the head of his or her neighbour. When the music stops, the leader asks the person wearing the hat to do an action for everyone to copy. The activity resumes when the music starts again.

OBSERVATIONS
- It is preferable, if the leader can encourage this, that participants allow each other to place the hat on their heads rather than take it from each other.
- The speed of the music may well affect the way the hat is passed on.

VARIATIONS
- Other items can be passed around, such as a scarf, a glove, a jacket or a cloak.

56

50 Where are you?

PRINCIPAL AIM   To develop group awareness and concentration.

FURTHER AIMS
- To develop name recognition.
- To develop an individual's awareness within a group setting.

EQUIPMENT   A keyboard or recorded music. A room with plenty of hiding places.

NUMBERS   4 to 10.

BASIC MODEL   Everyone moves, marches or dances around the room to an energetic piece of music. When the music stops, everybody hides. The leader then sings (or says), 'Let's find . . . Alice/Freddie', and asks the group to leave their hiding places and find the one participant who remains hidden. Once the hidden person has been found, the music starts up again and the activity continues until all participants have been found.

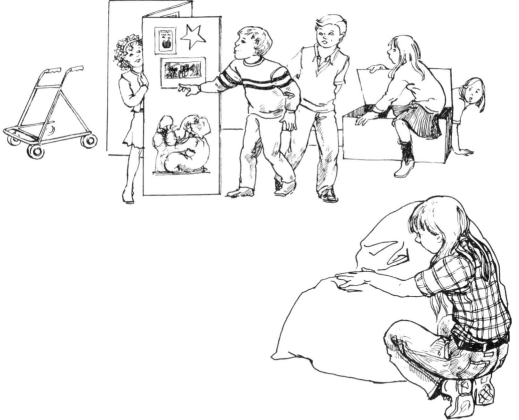

OBSERVATIONS
- Not all participants need to take part in the search every time. It is important, however, that they join in the dancing as soon as the music starts.
- The leader may need to encourage some participants to leave their hiding places rather than expect to be found every time.

51 *Watch the cymbal!*

PRINCIPAL AIM   To encourage social interaction.

FURTHER AIMS
- To encourage initiative.
- To encourage listening.
- To develop skills in taking turns.

EQUIPMENT   A large cymbal on a stand and a beater.

NUMBERS   4 to 6.

BASIC MODEL   The group sits in a close circle around the cymbal. The leader explains that the place where the beater strikes the cymbal will determine which participant plays next. One participant starts by striking the cymbal once. He or she then hands the beater to the person who is nearest to the place where the cymbal was struck. The beater continues to change hands in this way, with each player striking the cymbal once and then passing it on.

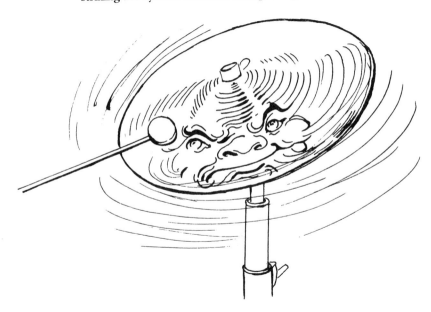

OBSERVATIONS
- The leader can encourage listening by ensuring that participants wait until the vibrations of the cymbal have stopped before they strike the cymbal again.
- If participants become restless the leader can ask them to do the activity as fast as possible.

VARIATIONS
- Instead of passing the beater on, each player can wait for the 'correct' person to ask for it.
- Another large instrument, such as the drum or a large bass xylophone, can be used.
- The instrument can be played with one hand instead of with a beater. Players have to watch very carefully.

52 *Heavy or sticky*

PRINCIPAL AIM   To encourage group co-operation.

FURTHER AIMS   • To develop imagination.
               • To increase self-confidence.

EQUIPMENT   One tambourine.

NUMBERS   4 to 8.

BASIC MODEL   The group sits in a circle. Participants pass the tambourine around the circle in silence and imagine that it is very heavy. The leader then suggests that the tambourine becomes sticky, smelly or slippery. The tambourine is put aside and an imaginary tambourine is passed around. This imaginary tambourine also becomes heavy or sticky, etc.

OBSERVATIONS   • Staff may wish to spark off ideas by, for example, nearly dropping the 'heavy' tambourine or getting the 'sticky' tambourine stuck to their clothes.

VARIATIONS   • Other small instruments can be used.
             • Participants can pass the instrument across the circle rather than around it.
             • A pretend 'mystery' instrument can be passed around. Participants can comment on what they think the instrument is once it has been around the circle.
             • A pretend instrument can be thrown around the circle.

53 Listen and walk!

PRINCIPAL AIM	To encourage group co-operation.
FURTHER AIMS	• To encourage concentrated listening. • To improve auditory discrimination. • To develop self-confidence.
EQUIPMENT	A blindfold.
NUMBERS	4 to 10.
BASIC MODEL	The leader blindfolds a volunteer. The aim of the activity is for that person to reach a chair at the other end of the room. One group member claps to encourage the person to move forwards; a second stamps to make him or her go backwards; a third makes clicking noises to make him or her side-step to the right; a fourth makes 'sh' noises to make him or her side-step to the left. Once the blindfolded person has found the chair, another volunteer takes his or her place.

OBSERVATIONS	• It helps if those who are encouraging forward and backward walking stand in front of and behind the blindfolded person. In the same way, the people encouraging right and left side-stepping should stand on appropriate sides. • The people making the noises have to listen to one another and co-operate well together. The blindfolded person needs to walk slowly and carefully and may need to hold someone's hand for reassurance.
VARIATIONS	• Instruments can be used instead of sounds. • The same person can make the different sounds for the different movements, selecting each sound appropriately. • Obstacles such as tables, bags or people lying on the floor can be put in the way of the blindfolded person's path to make the activity more challenging.

54 I like . . .

PRINCIPAL AIM   To encourage participants to interact with one another.

FURTHER AIMS
- To develop listening skills.
- To develop group awareness.
- To encourage self-assertiveness.

EQUIPMENT   One xylophone.

NUMBERS   4 to 10.

BASIC MODEL   The group sits in a circle. One participant has the xylophone and plays four notes. At the same time he or she says, 'I like Steven's/Jane's shoes'. The instrument is then passed to the left and the next person plays the xylophone and says what he or she likes about another participant. The activity continues until everyone has had a turn.

OBSERVATIONS
- Participants can discuss their different 'likes' at the end of the activity.
- Participants can play more than four notes or can play first and talk afterwards. This does not matter as long as each turn is fairly short and the focus of the playing is to support the spoken words.

VARIATIONS
- A range of different instruments can be used, with each participant making his or her own choice. In this case it is advisable to put each instrument aside after it has been used.
- Dislikes ('I don't like . . .') can also be expressed. Participants can also talk about different foods or activities they like or dislike.
- Instead of passing the instrument around the group in order, participants can pass it to the person about whom they have just given an opinion.

55 Hoop group

PRINCIPAL AIM To develop group co-operation.

FURTHER AIMS • To develop motor control.
• To encourage initiative.

EQUIPMENT As many hoops as there are participants. A keyboard or recorded 'slow marching' music.

NUMBERS 4 to 10.

BASIC MODEL Each participant chooses a hoop and 'hooks' one part of his or her body to another participant until the whole group is linked together with hoops. Once 'hooked up', the group stays quite still until the slow music starts and then tries to move as a group without coming apart.

OBSERVATIONS • The leader may need to give the group different ideas of how to link themselves to one another – using shoulders, arms, legs, heads, bodies, etc.

VARIATIONS • Participants can make a very small 'hoop group' with everyone clustered together, or a long 'hoop group' with everyone spread out. They can also use their imagination to make a 'spiky' group or a 'round' group.
• Small pieces of material (each about 20cm square) can be used instead of hoops. Participants can 'glue' people together (see 'Dance with a glued foot!' p. 86).
• Once the 'hoop group' is formed each child may be given a small portable instrument to play when the music starts.

56 *Catch my eye!*

PRINCIPAL AIM To develop eye contact.

FURTHER AIMS
- To encourage group co-operation.
- To increase concentration and listening.

EQUIPMENT An instrument for each participant.

NUMBERS 4 to 10.

BASIC MODEL The group sits in a circle, each participant with an instrument. The leader begins playing his or her instrument and after a short while looks up at a participant, inviting him or her to join in. After playing for a while, that participant looks up at another group member who then joins in the playing. This process continues until the whole group is playing together.

OBSERVATIONS
- It is helpful for the leader to have a melodic instrument whilst the others have percussion instruments.
- It may be necessary to begin with all the instruments (except the leader's) on the floor and for individuals to pick them up as they join in the playing.

VARIATIONS
- The leader alone can use eye contact to invite participants to join in.
- The leader can help people to be aware of the eye contact by singing their names at the appropriate moment.

57 Tap-a-back

PRINCIPAL AIM   To develop group co-operation.

FURTHER AIMS   • To increase tactile awareness and tolerance of physical contact.
               • To develop patience.
               • To develop concentration.

EQUIPMENT   None.

NUMBERS   4 to 8.

BASIC MODEL   The players sit in a circle and turn to face the person on the left. Inevitably, each person looks at the back of the person in front. The leader taps the back of the person next to him or her and this person, in turn, passes on the same type of tap. The activity continues all around the circle.

OBSERVATIONS   • Group members should keep quiet and concentrate on the 'message' being passed around.
               • Tapping may be with either one or two hands.
               • The activity works well if players close their eyes.

VARIATIONS   • A specific number of taps can be passed around.
             • A group participant can start the tapping.
             • A 'drawn' shape, cross or letter can be passed on.
             • Players can tap different parts of the back.

58 Red-handed

PRINCIPAL AIM To develop patience and co-operation.

FURTHER AIMS
- To increase awareness of others.
- To develop listening skills.
- To develop leadership skills.
- To work on colour recognition.

EQUIPMENT One large drum on a stand. Stickers or paints suitable for hands or fingernails.

NUMBERS 3 or 4.

BASIC MODEL Each participant places a hand on the drum, keeping it still. On the back of each hand is a different coloured paint mark or sticker. One person acts as 'caller' and names one hand to play, e.g. 'yellow hand' and that hand plays once. The caller then names another colour and the activity continues.

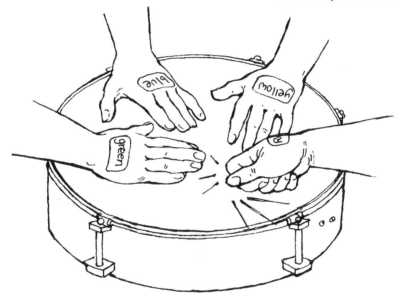

OBSERVATIONS
- Participants may need time initially to play the drum all together so as not to become impatient while listening to the caller.
- The caller can participate by having one 'coloured' hand on the drum.
- The caller can indicate loud or quiet playing by giving the instruction loudly or quietly.

VARIATIONS
- Both hands can be used, coloured either differently or the same.
- Colours can be duplicated, with two or more members playing at the same time.
- Several fingernails or fingers can be painted different colours.
- Participants can place their hands on their knees instead of on the drum when they are not playing. The caller needs to remember which colours have been used.

59 *Please interrupt!*

PRINCIPAL AIM   To encourage listening and patience.

FURTHER AIMS   • To develop group co-operation.
                • To develop initiative.

EQUIPMENT   An instrument for each participant.

NUMBERS   3 to 8.

BASIC MODEL   The group sits in a circle, each participant holding an instrument. One person plays alone until the person on their right interrupts by playing too. As soon as the first player is interrupted, he or she should stop and allow the other person to continue playing. That player continues until the next participant on the right interrupts, and so on.

OBSERVATIONS   • The leader may need to encourage the group to allow each player to have some uninterrupted playing time.

VARIATIONS   • Participants can interrupt each other at random rather than go around the circle.
              • A large instrument such as a drum or a cymbal can be placed in the middle of the circle and participants play and 'interrupt' one another on this, either with beaters or with their hands.

IV   Activities to develop motor control

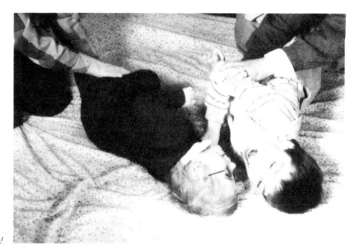

Roll to say hello!

Lead the leader!

60 Up and down

PRINCIPAL AIM   To develop concentration and listening skills.

FURTHER AIMS
- To develop motor control and spatial awareness.
- To encourage vocalization.
- To develop the concept of up and down.

EQUIPMENT   None.

NUMBERS   3 to 10.

BASIC MODEL   The group sits in a circle, holding hands. The leader waits for silence and then begins to make a vocal sound which gradually rises in pitch. At the same time the leader slowly raises his or her hands, encouraging the group to do likewise. Once all hands are up, the leader makes the same sound in reverse and everyone lowers their hands.

(Tune: *The Skye boat song*)

OBSERVATIONS
- The leader should begin this activity with very slow movements.
- Group members can join in with the vocal sounds if the leader wishes.
- The position of the hands can be emphasized by singing 'up' or 'down'.

VARIATIONS
- The words 'up' and 'down' can be sung, rather than using the vocal sound.
- Songs or parts of songs with rising or descending phrases can be used when sung slowly. For example, 'The Skye boat song' or 'The first Noël'.
- The activity can be done with eyes closed.
- The sliding pitch can change direction at any time.
- The group can hold onto a large hoop or a piece of rope placed in the centre while moving arms up and down.
- Actions such as 'tickle your toes' or 'tap your head' can be incorporated when arms are 'down' or 'up'.
- The activity can be done in pairs, with partners facing one another and holding hands.
- The whole body, or parts of the body, can move according to the sound.
- Instruments such as bells or tambourines that can be held and shaken simultaneously by two people can be used.
- The group can do the activity without holding hands.

61 Clap and sway!

PRINCIPAL AIM	To develop motor control.
FURTHER AIMS	• To develop concentration. • To develop listening skills. • To develop recognition of different body parts.
EQUIPMENT	None.
NUMBERS	3 to 10.
BASIC MODEL	Group members clap hands whilst the leader sings appropriate words to the tune of 'Who's afraid of the big bad wolf?' For example, 'Everybody clap your hands, clap your hands, clap your hands . . .' (see tune). At the end of the verse the leader sings the song at half speed with a lilting rhythm and changes the words to, 'Everybody sway like trees, sway like trees, sway like trees . . .'. These two versions of the song may be repeated in sequence as many times as required.

(Tune: *Who's afraid of the big bad wolf?*)

OBSERVATIONS	• The group may be more attentive if there is a slight pause between each verse.
VARIATIONS	• After a few verses the tune can be used without the words, with the leader encouraging appropriate actions. • Other actions such as foot stamping and head nodding can be tried. • Participants can suggest actions for this activity. • Participants can do some actions in pairs, e.g. tapping each other's knees or clapping each other's hands. • The leader can change the words of the song in order to use the activity for the naming of body parts.

62 *Shake it off!*

PRINCIPAL AIM   To develop motor control.

FURTHER AIMS   To improve listening skills; to develop anticipation and patience.

EQUIPMENT   Small pieces of different coloured material, each about 20cm square. Enough of these for each group participant to have at least one.

NUMBERS   3 to 10.

BASIC MODEL   Each participant chooses a square of material and puts it on his or her head as though it was a hat. The group leader then sings, 'We are wearing different coloured hats!' several times and ends up by singing, 'Shake, shake, shake them off!' (see tune below) while shaking his or her head until the piece of material falls off. All group members shake their pieces of material off at the same time. (The tune 'London Bridge is falling down' can also be used for this purpose.)

Repeat ad lib.

OBSERVATIONS
- Participants should not use their hands to help the pieces of material off.
- Some may take longer than others to shake their piece of material off.
- The group should wait until all the pieces of material are shaken off before starting the activity again.

VARIATIONS
- The pieces of material can also be shaken off arms, feet, neck, hands, etc.
- Different coloured pieces of material can be used to match different coloured clothing.
- Those with, for example, red pieces of material can shake their heads first, and those with other colours later.
- Participants can finish by waving their pieces of material in the air.
- The 'shaking song' can be recited rather than sung. It can also be accompanied by the guitar, a keyboard, the tambourine or clapping.
- This activity can be followed by 'Scarecrow' (p. 35).

63 Flying saucer

PRINCIPAL AIM   To develop motor co-ordination.

FURTHER AIMS   • To improve reactions.
                • To develop concentration.

EQUIPMENT   One cymbal with a strap or on a string. As many beaters as there are
             participants.

NUMBERS   3 to 8.

BASIC MODEL   Participants place their chairs approximately two metres apart around the
               room and sit down, each holding a beater. The leader moves between the
               players, making the cymbal 'fly' like a flying saucer. The players hit the cymbal
               if it comes within striking distance. When they do so, the cymbal flies away in
               another direction.

OBSERVATIONS   • The leader should allow the cymbal to fly gracefully between hits so that
                  participants can enjoy the sound.
                • The leader can challenge the players by trying to slip the cymbal past them.

VARIATIONS   • A large chime bar or triangle (with metal beaters) can be used instead of
                the cymbal.
              • A player can indicate whom the cymbal should fly to next.
              • With a large number, participants can hold hands and jointly hold beaters.
                They then have to work closely together in order to aim for and hit the
                flying saucer.
              • Different group participants can make the cymbal fly.

64 Sleeping music

PRINCIPAL AIM   To improve the ability to relax.

FURTHER AIMS   • To develop group co-operation.
                    • To develop self-control.

EQUIPMENT   A xylophone and a drum.

NUMBERS   3 to 8.

BASIC MODEL   Participants sit in a circle around a person who has been chosen to play the instruments. He or she lulls the listeners to sleep by playing the xylophone in an appropriate manner. When everyone has settled and 'fallen asleep', the player wakes up the group by playing the drum. Another participant then takes over the instruments.

OBSERVATIONS   • The leader should encourage participants to close their eyes even if some find this difficult at first.
                    • It may be useful to separate the two instruments, placing the drum outside the circle. This reduces the temptation for participants to play both instruments at once.
                    • Players should wait as long as possible before waking the group.

VARIATIONS   • Other contrasting instruments can be used.
                    • Two participants can play, taking one instrument each.

65 *Musical feet*

PRINCIPAL AIM	To improve motor control.
FURTHER AIMS	• To develop patience. • To develop imagination and creativity.
EQUIPMENT	One large, old white sheet. Different colours of paint, diluted in buckets. A keyboard or two contrasting pieces of recorded music.
NUMBERS	4 to 6.
BASIC MODEL	The leader lays the sheet out on the floor, and one participant dips his or her feet in paint and moves across one side of the sheet in response to the rhythm of marching music. When the music stops, the participant also has to stop and stand still. Another participant then dips his or her feet in a different colour paint and jumps on the other side of the sheet to the sound of a jig, again stopping when the music stops. Those not walking on the sheet watch and join in by clapping. Once the paint has dried, individual participants can recreate the marching and jumping by following the different coloured footsteps on the sheet.

OBSERVATIONS	• The leader should encourage people to notice how different movements produce different footsteps.
VARIATIONS	• Different movements, such as skipping, large and small steps and tiptoeing, can be tried.

66 *Sleeping tambourine*

PRINCIPAL AIM To develop motor control and concentration.

FURTHER AIMS
- To develop group co-operation.
- To develop a sense of responsibility.

EQUIPMENT One tambourine.

NUMBERS 3 to 10.

BASIC MODEL The group sits in a circle. The leader picks up the tambourine very carefully and passes it to his or her neighbour without making a sound. Group members pass the 'sleeping tambourine' around the circle in such a way that no sound can be heard.

OBSERVATIONS
- The leader can encourage participants to watch the tambourine whilst waiting for their turn.
- This activity is a useful contrast to more active games.

VARIATIONS
- The direction in which the tambourine is passed around can be changed at any time.
- Other instruments, such as maracas or shakers, can be used.
- The group can pass two instruments around simultaneously.

67 *Musical hoops*

PRINCIPAL AIM   To develop listening skills.

FURTHER AIMS   • To speed up reactions.
                • To encourage group co-operation.

EQUIPMENT   As many hoops as there are participants. A keyboard or recorded music.

NUMBERS   3 to 10.

BASIC MODEL   The leader scatters the hoops on the floor of a large room. Participants walk, dance or run around the hoops as soon as the music starts. When the music stops, everyone must find a hoop to stand in.

OBSERVATIONS   • Participants should not walk in the hoops while the music is playing.
                • The leader should stop the music for long enough to give all participants time to find a hoop.

VARIATIONS   • The hoops can be placed in the centre of the room rather than scattered all over.
              • Small pieces of carpet or material can be used instead of hoops.
              • Half the number of hoops can be used. Each group member then has to share a hoop with another.
              • If the hoops are all placed close together, each group member can put a foot in (or on) two different hoops when the music stops.
              • Three different coloured hoops can be used and matched up with corresponding coloured handkerchiefs (or pieces of material). Each group member waves a handkerchief as he or she dances to the music. When the music stops, participants stand in hoops corresponding to the colour of their handkerchiefs.

68 Train journey

PRINCIPAL AIM   To encourage pre-verbal vocalization.

FURTHER AIMS   • To develop group co-operation.
                • To release energy in a controlled way.

EQUIPMENT   One train whistle.

NUMBERS   4 to 10.

BASIC MODEL   The group sits in a circle. One member has the train whistle. The leader begins the train journey by slowly rubbing the palms of his or her hands together whilst making the traditional 'chuff-chuff' sound of a train. The group joins in. The sound begins slowly and rhythmically and then gradually increases in speed. When the 'train' reaches maximum speed, the whistle is blown. This indicates to the group that the train should begin to slow down gradually until it reaches the station and hisses to a standstill.

OBSERVATIONS   • This activity is more challenging and exciting the slower it begins.

VARIATIONS   • If no train whistle is available a volunteer can make the sound vocally.
              • Participants can rub hands on knees instead of just hands.
              • Other sound effects can be added. For example, doors opening, brakes, guard's whistle, etc.

69 *Listen and run!*

PRINCIPAL AIM   To co-ordinate listening skills with fast physical reactions.

FURTHER AIMS
- To speed up reactions.
- To encourage group co-operation.

EQUIPMENT   Several large percussion instruments such as drums or cymbals; one instrument per participant. A keyboard or recorded music.

NUMBERS   3 or 4.

BASIC MODEL   The leader places the percussion instruments in different corners of a large room, as far away from each other as possible. When the music starts, each participant finds an instrument and begins to play. When the music stops, everyone runs to a different instrument and waits for the music to start before playing again.

OBSERVATIONS
- Participants should put their beaters down on or next to their instruments before they start running.
- Quiet as well as loud music should be played in order to encourage listening.

VARIATIONS
- Smaller instruments can be used if they are placed on small tables or chairs.
- One of the participants can direct the activity by blowing a whistle to indicate that it is time to change instruments.

70 *Roll to say hello!*

PRINCIPAL AIM
To develop the ability to roll over.

FURTHER AIMS
• To encourage social interaction; to develop tactile awareness.

EQUIPMENT
One large mat or a thick carpet to lie on.

NUMBERS
4 to 10.

BASIC MODEL
Participants lie on their backs on the mat, forming a circle with their heads in the middle. Singing the song below, each participant rolls over to the side (or is helped to roll over) and stretches out to touch and greet his or her neighbour, who has also rolled over. After the greeting, everyone rolls over to the other side and says 'hello' to that neighbour. Participants then change places before starting the song and the actions again with new neighbours.

(Tune: *Five little speckled frogs*)

OBSERVATIONS
• It may be necessary to clarify the direction in which each participant should roll before starting the song.
• The leader may need to slow down or speed up the song depending on how fast participants are moving.

VARIATIONS
• Participants can touch their neighbours' faces, hands or arms once they have rolled over.
• Participants can hold a small instrument, such as the bells, and play for their neighbours once they have rolled over.

71 Copy my dance!

PRINCIPAL AIM   To develop the ability to observe and imitate.

FURTHER AIMS
- To develop physical co-ordination.
- To explore different types of movement and dance.
- To develop initiative and self-confidence.
- To develop eye contact and concentration.

EQUIPMENT   A keyboard or recorded dance music.

NUMBERS   6 to 10.

BASIC MODEL   Group members dance around freely to the music. The leader observes the group for a few minutes and then stops the music. He or she then suggests that everyone should dance in the way that one particular member has been dancing. That dancer demonstrates what he or she was doing and then the group dances to the music again in that particular style. The leader then picks out another person's style of dancing and this again is imitated by the group. The activity continues until all those who wish to demonstrate a particular style of dance have had the opportunity to do so.

OBSERVATIONS
- The leader can introduce this activity by first encouraging participants to imitate his or her own movements to recorded music.
- The leader can pick out very simple movements (such as nodding) or more complex movements (such as a sequence of three or four steps) for the group to imitate.

VARIATIONS
- Group members can explore certain types of movements, such as 'jerky movements', 'flowing movements', 'spiky movements' or 'round movements'. Different styles of music should be used to accompany these movements.
- The group leader can suggest that participants use their imagination to explore movements such as 'swaying trees', 'trumpeting elephants', 'wriggling snakes' or 'flying birds'.
- Participants can explore movements in pairs.

72 Concerto

PRINCIPAL AIM   To develop motor control.

FURTHER AIMS
- To develop self-confidence.
- To develop group co-operation.
- To encourage patience.

EQUIPMENT   A tambourine or a tambour for each participant except one. A keyboard or recorded music.

NUMBERS   4 to 10.

BASIC MODEL   One participant is invited to be the soloist and stands in the middle of the circle. The others all have tambours or tambourines. When the music begins, the participants dance around the soloist, playing their instruments. Meanwhile the solo player stands still. The music stops suddenly and the participants stand like statues, holding their instruments out in any position they choose. The solo player then goes around and plays all the instruments, one after another. When he or she has finished playing, the music and the activity start again with a new soloist.

OBSERVATIONS
- The soloist can be chosen by the previous one.
- The dancers can use the whole room rather than keeping to a circle.

VARIATIONS
- Two participants can be soloists simultaneously.
- Other portable instruments that can be tapped may be used.
- The leader may play a contrasting piece of music to accompany the soloist.

73 *Breaking the sound barrier*

PRINCIPAL AIM   To co-ordinate listening skills with fast physical reactions.

FURTHER AIMS
- To provide an opportunity for energy release.
- To encourage group co-operation.
- To develop concentration.
- To develop spatial awareness.

EQUIPMENT   A cymbal on a stand.

NUMBERS   4 to 6.

BASIC MODEL   The leader places a chair at one end of the room. The group waits by the cymbal at the other end of the room. One player prepares to run whilst another is poised to strike the cymbal (once, loudly). The moment it is struck, the runner races towards the chair, round it, and back to the instrument. Breathless, he or she has to sit down and listen if the cymbal is still resonating. Each person participates in turn.

OBSERVATIONS   The whole group should listen to the sound dying away, without touching the instrument.

VARIATIONS
- Other instruments that resonate well, such as the autoharp, the metallophone or chime bars, can be used. When using chime bars, the leader should select as low a note as possible; the sound resonates for longer.
- The runner can identify which one of two chime bars was struck.
- The runner can strike the instrument before starting to run.

74 *Over the rainbow*

PRINCIPAL AIM   To develop motor control.

FURTHER AIMS
- To develop group co-operation.
- To develop colour recognition and memory.

EQUIPMENT   Small pieces of yellow, red, blue and green material, each about 20cm square. A keyboard or recorded music.

NUMBERS   4 to 10.

BASIC MODEL   Each participant chooses a yellow, red, blue or green piece of material and places it on his or her head. The leader places a different coloured piece of material in each corner of the room. When the music starts, everyone dances, making sure that the material does not fall off. When the music stops, participants group in the appropriate colour corner of the room. Pieces of material may then be swapped around and the activity starts up again.

OBSERVATIONS
- The leader may need to remind participants which colour material they have on their heads.

VARIATIONS
- Participants can balance the pieces of material on their arms, shoulders, hands, etc.
- The leader can suggest running or jumping instead of dancing in order to increase the challenge of balancing the pieces of material.
- Participants can dance in pairs.

75 *Lead the leader!*

PRINCIPAL AIM   To develop motor control.

FURTHER AIMS
- To increase confidence in the ability to lead.
- To increase concentration.
- To learn to associate a code with an action.
- To speed up reactions.

EQUIPMENT   Bells, a drum, a cymbal and some beaters. A table to put the bells and beaters on.

NUMBERS   3 to 6.

BASIC MODEL   The leader arranges the instruments side by side, with the bells and the beaters within easy reach on a table. He or she then explains that different movements are associated with each of the instruments. Head shaking, for example, can be associated with the bells, lifting arms up with the cymbal, and jumping with the drum. A participant then plays the instruments one at a time. The leader sits or stands opposite the player and does the actions as the instruments are played. Other group members then take turns.

OBSERVATIONS
- It may be helpful to experiment with different movements before starting. See, for example, 'Copy my dance!' (p. 79).

VARIATIONS
- One participant can do the actions while another plays the instruments.
- The whole group can do the actions while one person plays the instruments.
- Different instruments and movements can be used.
- Three participants can each play an instrument.

76 Moving chairs

PRINCIPAL AIM   To co-ordinate movements with listening skills.

FURTHER AIMS
- To develop quick reactions.
- To encourage group co-operation.

EQUIPMENT   Several strong but easily moved chairs, one for each participant. A keyboard or recorded music.

NUMBERS   3 or 4.

BASIC MODEL   The participants sit on chairs in a row in a large empty room. When the music starts, they walk forward, still holding on to the front of their chairs with both hands. When the music stops, they stop and sit down.

OBSERVATIONS
- Participants should listen to the music being played and walk quickly or slowly depending on how fast the music is.
- Participants should be careful not to bump into one another or walk too closely to one another.

VARIATIONS
- The leader can give short instructions every time the music stops, suggesting that participants walk backwards, sideways, etc.
- Participants can also swap chairs, walk around their chairs, stand on them, etc.

77 *Mirror image*

PRINCIPAL AIM   To improve motor control.

FURTHER AIMS
- To increase concentration.
- To develop imagination.
- To develop observation skills.

EQUIPMENT   Two maracas. A keyboard or recorded dance music.

NUMBERS   4 to 10.

BASIC MODEL   Two participants stand facing one another, each holding a maraca in opposite hands. The remaining participants watch and listen. The soloists determine which of the two of them is going to lead. When the music starts, the leader moves the maraca, and his or her partner copies the movements as exactly as possible as though he or she were a mirror image of the leader. When the music stops, the soloists both stand still. When the music starts again, the two soloists either exchange leadership or two new soloists have a turn.

OBSERVATIONS
- The group leader may need to encourage the soloists to start off with slow movements.
- It may help to say that, whatever movements are made, the two soloists must always be able to see each other.
- As maracas are quite delicate it is sensible to have a rule that they must never touch anything else.

VARIATIONS
- Other small instruments, such as tambourines or castanets, can be used.
- One participant can stand opposite the whole group and invite everyone to imitate his or her movements.
- Different types of dance music can be tried.

85

78 Dance with a glued foot!

PRINCIPAL AIM   To develop motor control.

FURTHER AIMS
- To develop group co-operation.
- To develop confidence in leadership.

EQUIPMENT   Small pieces of different coloured material, each about 20cm square, one for each participant. A keyboard or recorded dance music of different styles.

NUMBERS   4 to 10.

BASIC MODEL   Each person chooses one piece of material and finds a special place on the floor for it. He or she then places one foot on the material and is 'glued' to the floor. Music is played and participants dance in whatever way they like, but keeping one foot 'glued' to the floor. The group leader observes the various styles of dancing and invites an individual to demonstrate his or her style of dance so that everyone else can imitate it. Participants then imitate a range of different dance styles.

OBSERVATIONS
- The leader may need to remind participants about their 'glued' foot.
- Participants should keep still and quiet when the music stops.

VARIATIONS
- Other parts of the body, such as knees or hands, can be 'glued' to the floor.
- Participants can use hoops instead of pieces of material if a large room is available. They can then be 'glued' either to the side of the hoop or to the space inside the hoop.
- It may be suitable to follow this activity by 'Make up your dance!' (p. 42).

Index to aims

Keywords to the aims of the activities are listed on the left in alphabetical order. The number of each activity relevant to that aim is written next to the keyword. An asterisk indicates that it is the principal aim of that activity.

Anticipation   6, 40, 42*
Auditory discrimination   5, 15*, 20, 21, 24, 47, 53
Awareness   2, 14, 22*, 37, 40*, 49, 50*, 54, 58

Body parts (recognition)   27, 61

Caring   49
Choice   23*, 24, 48
Colour (recognition)   58, 74
Communication (non-verbal)   33, 38
Concentration   1, 2*, 3, 4, 5*, 6, 8*, 9*, 13*, 14*, 15, 17*, 18, 20*, 21*, 23, 27, 32, 41, 49, 50*, 56, 57, 60*, 61, 62, 66*, 73, 77
Confidence   24, 36*, 75
Co-operation   3, 4, 5, 7, 8, 9, 11, 17, 19, 20, 21, 25, 28, 29*, 31, 32, 34, 43*, 44*, 45, 46*, 48*, 49*, 52*, 53*, 55*, 56, 57*, 58*, 59, 64, 66, 67, 68, 69, 72, 73, 74, 76, 78
Co-ordination   10, 12, 19, 63*, 76*
Creativity   9, 36, 65

Direction (a sense of)   14

Empathy   16, 37*
Energy release   5, 12, 42, 68, 73
Eye-contact   22, 33, 35*, 38, 47, 56*, 72

Imagination   11, 16, 52, 65, 77
Imitation   71*
Initiative   2, 24*, 26*, 28*, 32, 34*, 35, 38*, 46, 51, 55, 59, 71
Interaction   5, 51*, 54*, 70

Leadership   30, 31*, 33, 58, 75, 78
Listening   1*, 2*, 3*, 4*, 5*, 6*, 7*, 8*, 9*, 10*, 11*, 12*, 13*, 14*, 15*, 16*, 17*, 18*, 19*, 27, 28, 31, 32, 34, 35, 36, 37, 38, 39, 41, 42, 43, 44, 46, 51, 53, 54, 56, 59*, 60*, 61, 62, 67, 69*, 75, 76*
Locating sound   4*

Memory   16*, 18, 20, 48, 74
Mobility   35, 71
Motivation   26*, 30
Motor control   15, 19, 29, 39, 43, 55, 60, 61*, 62*, 65*, 66*, 70*, 72*, 74*, 77*, 78*

Names (recognition)   2, 22, 50

Observation   2, 9, 20, 30, 34, 37, 40, 71*, 77

Patience   3, 6*, 11, 19*, 22, 23, 25, 26, 27, 29, 36, 45, 57, 58*, 59*, 62, 65, 72
Preparation (for a group outing)   11
Pre-writing skills   10

Reactions (speeding up)   1*, 12, 21, 34, 44, 63, 67, 69*, 73*, 75, 76
Relating sound to movement   15, 47, 73*, 75, 76*
Relaxation   6*
Responsibility   49, 66

Self-assertiveness   54
Self-confidence   7, 8, 25*, 29, 30*, 32*, 33, 40, 43, 52, 53, 71, 72
Self-control   26, 45*, 64
Self-esteem   39
Sharing   39*, 46*
Sitting control   39
Spatial awareness   12, 60, 73

Tactile awareness   27*, 57, 70
Taking turns   7, 40*, 41*, 51
Tolerance   27, 57
Trust   13

Vocalization   12, 31*, 60, 68*

Cross-reference table

Alphabetical list of activities	No instruments needed (excluding keyboard or recorded music).	Only one instrument needed (excluding keyboard or recorded music).	Keyboard (or recorded music) required.	Additional equipment required.	Activities involving art.	Unsuitable for 'non-mobile', wheelchairs. *	Suitable only for four or fewer participants.	Number of activity.
All change!			✓			✓		44
Back to back								7
Bells and tambourines			✓			✓		9
Big Ben								19
Breaking the sound barrier		✓				✓		73
Catch my eye!								56
Catch a rhythm!	✓							18
Circle the drum!		✓				✓		32
Clap and sway!	✓							61
Clap and tap!		✓						34
Come and get it!		✓				✓		35
Concerto			✓			✓		72
Conductor			✓					33
Contrary motion	✓							8
Copy my dance!			✓			✓		71
Dance and change!			✓			✓		46

Activity						Number
Dance with a glued foot!	✓			✓		78
Ding or dong	✓			✓		21
Farewell symphony		✓				45
Find the leader!			✓			2
Flying saucer		✓		✓		63
Growing flowers		✓		✓	✓	30
Guess who!					✓	37
Hands up!		✓				1
Hat dance	✓	✓		✓		49
Heavy or sticky			✓	✓		52
Hello!			✓			22
Hoop group	✓	✓		✓	✓	55
Humpty's downfall	.					42
Hunt the sweet!	✓		✓			17
I like			✓			54
Kings and queens of the bells			✓			43
Lead the leader!		✓		✓		75
Listen and choose!		✓		✓		24
Listen and remember!			✓			16
Listen and run!		✓		✓	✓	69
Listen and walk!	✓	✓		✓	✓	53
Listen, dance and paint!	✓	✓		✓	✓	15
Make me dance!	✓	✓		✓		40
Make up your dance!		✓		✓	✓	36
Mirror image		✓				77
Motor-biking			✓		✓	12

* 'Non-mobile' indicates that the person in the wheelchair is unable to move the wheelchair on his or her own.

Alphabetical list of activities

Activity	No instruments needed (excluding keyboard or recorded music).	Only one instrument needed (excluding keyboard or recorded music).	Keyboard (or recorded music) required.	Additional equipment required.	Activities involving art.	Unsuitable for 'non-mobile' wheelchairs. *	Suitable only for four or fewer participants.	Number of activity.
Moving chairs	✓		✓			✓	✓	76
Moving mouse		✓		✓				27
Musical feet	✓		✓	✓	✓	✓		65
Musical hoops	✓		✓	✓		✓		67
Musical lines	✓			✓	✓			10
Mystery notes		✓						20
Name game	✓							31
Over the rainbow	✓		✓	✓		✓		74
Peace-lovers and warriors								5
Pied piper		✓		✓		✓		13
Please interrupt!								59
Pop! goes the instrument		✓		✓				23
Quiet and loud			✓					6
Red-handed				✓	✓		✓	58
Roll or throw!				✓				47
Roll to say hello!	✓			✓				70

90

Activity						No.
Scarecrow	✓			✓		29
Sending messages	✓			✓		41
Shake it off!	✓			✓		62
Sleeping music						64
Sleeping tambourine		✓	✓			66
Solo time		✓	✓			25
Sound effects						11
Swaying hoops	✓	✓		✓		39
Tap-a-back	✓	✓				57
The empty chair					✓	38
Time bomb	✓			✓	✓	4
Train journey	✓			✓		68
Twirling tambourine		✓				26
Up and down	✓	✓				60
Watch the cymbal!	✓	✓				51
What now?	✓	✓		✓		48
Where are the bells?	✓	✓				3
Where are you?	✓	✓			✓	50
Where shall I play?		✓			✓	28
Which way?		✓				14

* 'Non-mobile' indicates that the person in the wheelchair is unable to move the wheelchair on his or her own.